This Notebook Belongs To:

____

Made in United States
North Haven, CT
21 January 2024

47729602R00067